Steph

I just wanted to say
thank you for being such
a big part of this book's
journey and successes.
I appreciate your _light_
+ I'm sending you so much
love ♡
    — Angélica

P.S. I'm so sorry, I'm at the
post office now and I started
signing this on a wet table so
this libro will probably have some
water damage, but I thought it was
        still worth sending!

they

call

me.

they call me.

by
angélica maria

ALEGRIA
PUBLISHING

davina@alegriamagazine.com

ISBN: 978-1-7379927-1-4

Published by Alegria Publishing
Book cover and layout by Sirenas Creative

they call me.

**Poems in this book have been published in the
following collections:**

"They Call Me Chismosa" — *The LatinX Poetry
Project by Alegria Publishing*

"In Critique of Modesty" — *You Don't Have to Be
Everything: Poems for Girls Becoming Themselves* by
Workman Publishing

"The Red Dress" — *The BreakBeat Poets, Vol. 4:
LatiNEXT* by Haymarket Publishing

angélica maria

Acknowledgements

for the mujeres that have taught me the importance of unbecoming.
thank you Lina, for being a sister, friend and healer in my life again
and again.
thank you to my tias in the U.S and in Juarez, that show me there is
no such thing as a good woman, just what a woman decides to be.
thank you to my poetry communities in different parts of the world,
that make me brave enough
to share what I find to be true.
thank you to my mom and my sister, whose own healing journey
continually inspires my own.
thank you to my dad, El Don Juan, who shows me you can face the
worst of life and still plant your flowers.
thank you to the past lovers that did not work out, that cracked me
open and made me find myself in order to redefine myself.
thank you to Alegria for believing in the words and being the perfect
family for this new born baby.
thank you to Stephanie for making these words presentable.

angélica maria

contents

l. anger | el enojo

ll. sexuality | la sexualidad

lll. love | el amor

IV. reclamation | la reclamación

They Call Me

party girl/ shy girl/ crazy girl/ quiet girl/ american girl/ exotic girl/ poor
girl/ priveledged girl/ little girl/ grown girl/ smart girl/ dumb girl/ easy
girl/ prude girl/ hairy girl/ pretty girl/ good haired girl/ messy haired
girl/ city girl/ working girl

they call me by every name except my own

&

it takes me years
to learn
to answer
to none of them

angélica maria

they call me.

1. anger | el enojo

angélica maria

Unlearning Anger

When I was 8 years old, I pushed my brother to the pavement and beat him up in front of his friends with my two little fists. The group of boys was making fun of me, so I entered into a special kind of rage that I had never experienced before. Once tears flooded my brother's eyes, I was told that this was an unacceptable thing to do, that little girls cannot fight boys in this way—or anyone, for that matter.

Respectfully, I normally do not believe in choosing violence. However, looking back, I am deeply proud of that little 8-year-old girl, who felt threatened and angry that she was being made fun of, and decided to act upon her anger. I think of all the times girls are taught to be polite before making sure we are safe, to be quiet before being confrontational, to silence ourselves if that means making others comfortable.

All my life, I watched men throw temper tantrums while women watched, pledging allegiance to silence. The world taught me that I was allowed to watch anger, to absorb anger, to be a punching bag for anger, but never to inhabit it.

Beginning

I believe all anger started
 once as a cry
until it was forced to become

a scream

Wildfire

how beautiful is rage,
the same way a wildfire is beautiful
the same way the reds & oranges swallow
the air & force us to marvel in its dance

of course if you try & control it
you will be burned instantly
it is hot to the touch

it is meant to expand, grow
it is meant to be seen,
it is meant to put on a show
to crackle and scream and glow

it is meant to remind us
that we all carry within us
a spark that is capable of engulfing
forests in their entirety

if we choose to use it

They Call Me Chismosa

they call me *chismosa* or *gossiping woman*

because I have stories instead of manners
dreams instead of children

"chismoooossaaaaaa"
the word casts a spell around itself
wakes silence in the night
with a sharpened machete

opposite of a chismosa:
a muñeca
the porcelain painted doll in the dining room cupboard
a girl with lips sealed so tight
she woke up one day
and forgot how to speak

I, however, was born screaming
& never quite learned how to stop

I escaped from my cardboard box long ago
and never could
go back

they call me *chismosa*
and I say
"thank you, I have dedicated years to the craft"

if I had a nickel for every time a man spoke over me
I could even out the wage gap
I could rent a recording studio, and start my own chismosa podcast
I could buy out all the rows of plastic girls in the store aisle
and crack them open
& when news breaks
that another maria is kidnapped in my town

I do not sit still on a shelf
I buy a megaphone
open the chamber of my mouth,
spit the slicked saliva gasoline

they call me.

into the ether
&
set the city ablaze
before silence swallows another

chismosa you call me
because you know you cannot kill a woman with more
language than fear

because you know a mouth
with a story,
and the nerve to tell it,

lives
forever.

The Cat Call

who would have thought
you:
furry creature of teeth and muscle
could walk down a mundane street corner
and ignite a circus,
turning a slew of sitting men into jumping monkeys
just like that?

but to be fair,
have you seen yourself?
legs built of ancient muscle
move swift and seamless
every cell in sync with the rhythm of your step
and you
act so unaware
of your own brilliance

feline fatale does not turn her head to the "cat call"
who would a lion be to spend time entertaining
field mice?

you walk with jaguar pride
heart thumping loudly
body made of water and dry desert
silent and methodical
thick fangs thirsty for a real meal
eyes set on game much larger
have you ever heard the cat call, call back?

the sound made
at the consumption of a chosen victim
of the roar that permeates
from the bottom of a
lioness' belly

that noise, so large it
creeps into the ear of a red ant
makes a bustling jungle, an erupting street corner of
men
in an instance,

deafeningly
still.

they call me.

after Barbie makes a Frida Kahlo doll,
and paints her with two separate eyebrows

Ode to Frida Kahlo's Unibrow

all hail you, rebel caterpillar, activist of the body
signed yourself in ink between two temples
and taught the world what art is
you front-row student
know-it-all
hands reaching high, begging to be seen

you spectacle of art critic theory
stealer of the spotlight
sexy slicked upright and
   lista pa la foto

you, fiber fists
a million middle fingers pointed to the male gaze
you who makes a mockery of a razor

you soil to seed
harvest and hopeful
garden of mujer
rise up over bikini line
over top lip
over barbed wire, and cement wall

you revolutionary without even trying
a million flags staked and waving
antique bridge of agency and body
rustic body of country
prickly continent of homeland, watched its kin graze
itself away for the colonizer
stand unsplit and unmoving
lush brown and full
say
"take me whole, or do not take me at all"

say

"keep your ready blade
     far away
        from me."

Mi Princesa

"mi princesa" my dad would call me
but he and I knew he did not mean a Cinderella type of princess

my dad meant a Cihuacotl Aztec type of princess,
a warrior princess, the other princesses
were always busy waiting to be saved
by a man
            by a miracle
                        by a narrative

I never believed in that kind of princess

Apa did not shield me from danger
or tell me that life is a fairytale
Apa told me:
"there is you, your hands, and a bloodthirsty world
I will not shield you, instead I will give you a knife
I will show you how to hold it
I will teach you that
you carry within you all you need to be victorious
and the day that anyone tries to step to you,

you will know what to do."

Quiet

in 2005, when the boys on the little league baseball team
make fun of me for being a girl
apá says, "mija, just show them that you are better than them
they will all shut up"

from then on, I run laps around the baseball field
every day until the sun goes down
with each step I imagine myself stronger
than the boys who laugh at me
I believe it is here that I first
fell in love with the quiet
with the rhythm of my own body
the completeness of it all
the boys begin to call me "tomboy"
but I do not care

the day of tryouts finally comes —
we have to sprint a home run
and I leave Timmy in the dust
the rest of the boys with their jaws wide open but nothing to say

here I find the quiet again
I take it in,
that sweet sweet
sound, the way it always
comes full circle

Evolving

thank you, enojo, anger
for protecting me
for shielding me
when i could not count on anyone else to do so

thank you for being my sword
my blazing machete
held by a shaking hand,
& a wounded heart

you have saved me
time & time again

I embrace you
I see you &
I am finding new ways
to keep myself safe

they call me.

11. sexuality | la sexualidad

angélica maria

Sacrifice

I am making love to a man I think I love. I think he loves me, I think he loves me in the way I think I turned the stove off before leaving the house; hopeful but terrified of dealing with the latter consequences. In the rhythm of us, I notice my necklace of La Virgen de Guadalupe swinging back and forth against my chest like a pendulum. I think I love this man, but I also think that I never had to think about whether or not I truly loved someone. That divine love never makes you use "think", and instead insists upon simply "knowing". Afterwards I stop and wonder if I just love the fact that he has chosen me. That in a room full of people something about his gaze felt holy. I stare at La Virgen de Guadalupe looking back at me, and I wonder what religion has taught me after all these years. That perhaps maybe the only reason I am here is because for years I was taught love meant sacrificing myself for a man in the hopes that one day he will accept me, call me graceful, that one day he will tell me

I am good.

angélica maria

Unlearning Good

I was called crazy the first time I referred to God as a "she". I thought it natural, that if the source of life has always come from a woman, then it would only be logical that the creator of life would also be a woman. Devoted Catholics, however, did not agree with my reasoning, and let me know that the idea was insulting. This was the first time I felt the voice of my inner niña slowly being silenced, shamed into oblivion. I stopped attending church when I was around 15, meaning I thought that I had turned that page of my life into a new blank chapter. What I actually found ahead of me was decades of unlearning, of re-writing my own narrative, one where the whole trinity of me: niña, woman, & diosa could finally exist fully & completely, as one.

An Ode to La Virgen de Guadalupe

my tia mounts La Virgen de Guadalupe high on the wall like some
families mount big-screen tvs / mexicans, both in the united states
and mexico, really lose it over La Virgen de Guadalupe / whenever my
uncle acted like a *pendejo* / my grandmother said he better crawl on
the ground to mexico and ask Our Lady for forgiveness / I remember
/ when a man I loved / told me that in chihuahua some traffickers pop
off the bottom of her statue and place cocaine inside the ceramic casing
to move the product into the u.s. / I fell in love/ with the idea that a
holy woman could also hide something dangerous inside of her/ at 17 I
came to the mantel and I told tia "I want to be just like her"/ she smiled
and held the palm of my hand / what tia did not know was that I didn't
mean I wanted to be like La Virgen in the saintly way / or the *virgen*
way / I meant in the way that La Virgen is as loved / as she is feared / I
meant the ease in which she brings a man to his knees / in front of her.

El Origen

a veces me siento débil
until I remember,

que la vida eterna
viene de entre mis piernas.

The Origin

sometimes I feel weak,
until I remember
the source of all creation,
including

the moon, the tides & sacred life
      comes
           from the meeting
                of my inner thighs.

"Losing it"

such a strange idea given to me
that the day I make love
for the first time
I am losing something

if my body is an instrument
the first time I make love
I become a symphony
I see all my different parts
become something completely
new
the rise and fall of my breath
like music notes
the strumming of secret spots
beget new sounds
the perfection of how
all my elements work together
to yield harmony

the first time I make love
I have lost *nothing*
I have gained a new world of
possibility

The Red Dress

what is it about a red dress,
that snaps a head back like an overstretched rubber band?

I only put on my red dress
when I want to be the bloodshot pool in the center of your iris
when I know there is nothing to lose
        only eyes to steal
        hours of time to put back into my dripping hourglass

slip the red dress on
and the night's heartbeat throbs at the nexus of my index finger
yeah, in the red dress   every move I make is photographed
each picture framed onto the fireplace of my exes
a rate of five hundred dollars is charged for each shot
and deposited directly into my bank account

with the money I buy
ten more red dresses
        and live two hundred more years

in the red dress   me mando yo
in the red dress every man that ever left me waiting
asks me to dance

in the red dress my mouth drops the word
"no"

like a glass of wine
on your favorite blouse

in the red dress
tears are a lake mirage to my pupils

I only laugh
to show the size of my teeth

in the red dress I hunger for oxygen like flame   engulf every
centimeter I find

they call me.

hell's honorable showpiece you can call me

here to bite back the night

here to claim everything stolen

mine.

Power

in my early twenties, for three years
I work as a bartender in a speakeasy

I learn the game of service
of winks & smiles
fake laughs & timing

the ultimate goal is tips

I mind my business and walk out
with hundreds of liquor-stained dollar bills
in my pockets every other night

the bank clerk calls me
"scandalous"
always stares at me suspiciously
like I know something he does not
like I harness an energy he cannot

I prefer the term *sorcerer,*
I prefer the term *magic woman,*
she who grins &
the universe yields to

Ode to Red Lipstick

ode to my favorite confidence booster
to dynamite in a gold tube
if hellbent was a color
it would be this shade
the one you reach for
when you're ready to walk into a room filled with your enemies

I love how she leaves a signature on
everything—
glass rims, napkins, necks
feminine graffiti

if looks could kill,
she would be the culprit
the chalk that outlines
the body at the crime scene

In Critique of Modesty

"hey girl, can we tone it down? less spanish, more sponsor-friendly?
what if we change the words around? we would never want to offend
anyone, of course"

a professor says I ought to try a more *modest* approach to writing,
a potential employer says I ought to dress more *modestly* for the job

what a meek cheering squad modesty has, I respond
what unenthused, half-committed fans I say

me,
I want to yell the way belligerent american men
do
I want to shoot my guns at the sky in honorship and scream
I want a festival in the streets
I want nationalism for being
yes yes yes
I want shirts with my own face on them
I want to be a bikini on a blonde white girl
I want schools to make children recite an allegiance to me each
morning
I want horns and a parade
please don't forget the fireworks
I want a song, plastic glitter stars scattered all over the pavement
I want to wave to you from space
I want to be staked on the front of someone's pickup truck
hoorah hoorah

what extraordinary freedom, what definite safety
to be seen everywhere

unafraid.

they call me.

angélica maria

lll. love | el amor

Unlearning Love

There was a time when I believed the most magical place to find love was in another person. This came from a combination of media, fairy tales, parental examples, and of course, narratives thrust upon me by the world.

The problem with this notion is, if the goal is to find love in another person, I must be willing to sacrifice myself in order to become what the other person wants. So without even realizing, I became a master at mirroring what I believed other people wanted me to be, in the hopes to one day receive that love. I later learned that this was self-betrayal.

The terrifying, but incredible realization on the other end of this, is that you are forced to realize all of the love you are searching for outside of yourself, is already yours to give.

Love Letter, Re-imagined

love letter where the sender is the same as the receiver

all doused in amor and forevers

love letter that does not get burned afterwards in a crying hysteria

when the relationship ends

love letter that does not end

love letter that is received with as much love as it is given

love letter written as a mantra, a psalm

love letter with vows deep as the author's eyes

& true as her heart

love letter for the most important relationship in the world;

the one between the author & herself.

they call me.

Wings

how could I speak of love
& not speak of wings?

not speak of butterflies
& the sensation of flying?

how could I speak of love
and not mention that
it wasn't until I let
myself fall, with complete abandon

that I realized I had any
wings at all?

Alas

¿cómo podría yo hablar de amor
y no hablar de las alas?
¿no hablar de las mariposas
y la sensación de volar?
¿cómo podría yo hablar de amor
y no mencionar que
no fue hasta que caí
y me dejé llevar por completo,
en esa nada del abismo,
cuando vi por primera vez, mis alas?

they call me.

Bloom

in México City,
all of the jacaranda trees bloom perfectly on time
there is no schedule or fixed plan
for a jacaranda tree to bloom
she follows
her ritmo, she knows when it is her time,
and when she does

the whole city just stares in awe

the same goes for you too

At the Mercado

señor victor picks all my fruit
he's had the same fruit stand
for 30 years in méxico city
so I trust that he knows best

he speaks of mangoes & maguey
like art enthusiasts speak of
paintings in new york

on sunday when I visit
I am in need of avocados
I ask victor to pick which
one he believes are best

before he leaves he tells me
"the bruised are the best ones,
because they are the softest inside"

I think to myself,
"I believe that is true for people too."

My Apá Does My Ponytails

combing curly hair is not for the faint of heart
my apá takes on the job because my mother
claims I get my curls from him

apá grew up between south central & chihuahua,
apá's hands learned fight, learned blood, learned clench
but did not learn tenderness
until me

maybe they resisted at first, but eventually they learned
how to slick baby hairs to perfection, how to tie a red ribbon
into a bow

it's beautiful to me what a man's hands can learn
outside of survival

La Sirena

como las olas
nadie le controla

a siren of love
se mete en problemas
porque no te puede soltar
si no es para siempre
ella no te va a amar

they didn't know that
her love was so deep,
depths that the ocean
couldn't even reach

Grow

how many nights have you looked for love
searched for love
waited for love
sacrificed yourself for love,
to never find what you were looking for?

but maybe love was never something outside
maybe it is something you grow into

maybe all that time that you were waiting
for love

love was waiting for you

Eterno

lo único eterno es lo interno,
recuerdo y vuelvo
recuerdo y vuelo

Eternal

the only eternal is the internal
I remember & I return
I remember & I fly

No Te Necesito

no te necesito,
if I was only here because I needed you
it would mean I didn't really love you

I want to try a love outside of need,
outside of filling my cup with your water,
outside of you being "my other half"

I want to erase all the ideologies of love
we learn from
las canciones de bachata y telenovelas

I want to show up ready,
I want to not use you as a crutch for my brokenness,
I want to not need you,

para poder amarte bien

Ode to the Heart

to that beautiful shape
the one we carve into tree trunks
& etch into
diaries

the world taught us it was
made of glass
something fragile
       to be shattered
something that breaks when
we give it away

those of us who have
loved, & lost love, know
that it really is a muscle:

it is in the tearing
that it grows stronger

Femenina Divina

en este mundo tan cruel,
llevo el corazón tatuado en la piel

y ¡que fortuna!
nacer con tanta dulzura
y esta noche sin duda
abajo de la luna
voy a amar con locura

They Call Me Gordita

as a niña, me gritaron "gordita"

"barriga llena, corazón contento",
decía mi papá

I had a panza & chubby cheeks
because my father grew up so poor
the only gifts his family gave him
fueron dulces y comida corriente

we give our children what we know
my father knew a hot meal
as cariño
he did not know health science
or nutrition
but knew plenty was better than
hungry

this too, I recognize as love

Maybe in Another Life You Do It All Right

you leave the party on time,
you do not kiss the bright-eyed boy or girl in the hallway,
you walk straight towards your car,
you say the right things when asked how you're doing
like a Siri device,
you do not melt your truth onto everyone like candle wax

you do not wear the red dress,
that drapes your curves like a greek statue
you put on the sweater your aunt picked out
you lie and say alcohol disgusts you,
that you could never even sniff the stuff without gagging
you put your hand over your mouth & pretend to do so
you choose a man you do not love
who owns a beautiful studio in manhattan & calls when he says he will

maybe you choose grad school instead of the trip to london
you put your money in property instead of late-night adventures &
alcohol
maybe you make your parents proud
& never see the world

maybe you choose this over the life
your every fiber reaches for
maybe you put the hummingbird of your heart
into a wire cage
place it behind all the winter coats & convince yourself her
screams are the wind

but in that case   what would perfect mean to you

if it did not give you a
single story
to leave behind?

Ode To Fernando Botero

because his sculptures & his paintings
look like women I know
they look like women I love

women that grew up around a stove top
& know recipes by heart
thick women
voluptuous women
hips bigger than their heart
& hearts bigger than
a dinner table

with stories that wrap around
the room like the aroma
of cafe de olla
eyes deeper than an olla
de tamal
wisdom beyond what
I am able to understand
today but still

I listen

Returning

one night I am laying in bed
tracing the different marks of
my body, embarking on a journey
of my own skin

I admire how each one has
a distinct shape
the way the stretch marks
on my legs resemble rivers

the scars on my back mirror
landmarks, small islands on an atlas
I would like to one day visit

I can't help but notice how
much my body resembles a map
the way one point always connects
back to another
the way that a story lives
behind each dot & shape

and I think of how many times
I felt the need to travel outside of myself,
eagerly looking for a place that felt
familiar, new and safe

only
to find
that I what I was searching for
for so long

was a way back
to myself

they call me.

El Perdón

I love you so deeply that
despite all the damage done,
I can forgive you

I love me so much
that because of all the damage done
 I will let you go

angélica maria

IV. reclamation | reclamación

They Call Me Bien Creida

"have you seen *esa chica*?

I swear she is so full of herself, *bien creida*,
I mean
                         who does she think she is?
she walks with that attitude
like she's royalty, like she owns the place, like
the cement sidewalk is a red carpet that unfolds in front of her
         I mean, where could she possibly be going?"
& of course I am not naive,
I hear every whisper that mentions my name on the sidewalk,
I hear them toss the phrase "full of herself" around like a sin,
so then
I ask myself,

what is it that they would prefer me to be?
Is empty not the opposite of full?
If given these options, which one would I choose for my own
daughter?
Is what they whisper of me in disgust, not all that I should aspire to
be?

so on monday, I wear the three-inch heels to the grocery store
I look like a walking money bag because frankly: I am
because I have earned every cent I put into myself

& when the señoras whisper with their raised eyebrows
"bien creida"
"she is so full of herself"

I take a moment & smile

because I know it to be true, because I know how
many nights I spent empty in order to teach
myself how to become full of
myself
full   of   myself
bien creida

that sounds like a song to me
like centuries of work
of unlearning shame

so of course I could never go back now
not after being so full,
después de creer tanto en mi,
jamás podría,

& I would never want to.

Ode To My Rizos / Curls

rambunctious ringlets
rebellious rulers of my cabeza
they called you frizzy
untamed
fluffy and wild

I call you mine
I call you divine

I call you righteous roots
of both my head &
my lineage
how they represent a past of
rebellion & growth

they remind me that one of the
most beautiful parts of us
is the part which refuses to back down

the part that will always fight
to live free
that will
always desire to live
　&
absolutely

untamed

Acentos

an accent is just a mother tongue
that refuses to let her child
go

La Exótica

"ooh, could you cook me latin food?"
a man laughs as he asks me

& of course I *could,*
but what makes him think he could handle
this spice?

my tapatío tongue, the kind made to
cleanse a body from the inside out

to him, I'm a white tiger
an amazonian snake
you know, something people love to try
to own
before it turns them into a meal

he says I look *exotic*, I say he looks like an easy dinner
like a tooth to add to my necklace of teeth. I mean,

doesn't he know the rules of the jungle?

how the most dangerous creatures are made beautiful
solely to entice their prey?
I flash him all my fangs
I bat my venus fly trap lashes

I show him how quickly the hunted can become the hunter

The Darkness Needs Your Fuego, Mija

that chispa, that spark
behind your chest, mija
it never goes out
even if it dwindles, a veces

the darkness, if only you see how it shows
off your light
how it draws the world's eyes
to your infinite flame

oh, how you glow
oh, how you never go
out

you, a light that guides lost
souls home
a warmth that roars against
this frigid world

I honor the flame in you
because I know it resembles the flame
in me,
too

I Hope I Die in This Dress

I tell my sister before we go out dancing

I'm not being dramatic, I actually love this dress
so much I could die in it
If I had to pick an outfit for my funeral,
It would be this one

what I really mean is, I hope I'm never caught seen
wearing anything I don't *absolutely* love
what I mean is, I spent so much time getting ready today
because I believe this life is completely precious
& and I want to show up for it,
savor it, drink it to the last sip

I want to put this life inside of a polaroid, a poem
somewhere where it can last forever
even when I'm no longer here to see it

what I really mean is, even if this life
is a janky house party, I'm dressing to the nines,
I'm putting my best foot forward,
I'm leaving nothing behind

They Call Me Bitch

"hey there little bitch!"

a man yells at you from a '97 Honda pickup truck. you are 13 years old & still wearing a training bra.

"yeah she's pretty and all, but she's too much of a bitch."

you are 16 and a waiter in an Irish pub tells you this about a waitress who asked the chef to stop slapping her ass at work.

"ain't that a bitch?"

17 years old: your alcoholic neighbor says about his wife who he abused for years when she finally found the courage to leave him.

"fine, you're ugly anyway. keep walking, bitch!"

18 years old, bus station in New York, no explanation needed.

the older I become,
the less I care about   being called a bitch
as much as I care about   becoming one

that is to say

what a woman becomes   when she retires
the burden of being nice

& becomes herself.

they call me.

Red Tie Event

side note:

it is said that in ancient times, our Aztec ancestors used to brush hot
colors upon their faces before entering into gruesome battles

in ciudad juárez, eight miles from my apartment,
tia carmen lives in a city where murder invades the night like a
swarm of bustling fireflies
& girls in their skirts and high heels are taken
            from the street in the lifespan of a   whisper

when she sits at her vanity still enough, you can hear
            a march erupting
                        the clinks of swords releasing from their cases

for the first time,
I notice the wrinkles   moving in over her face   like a fleet
of horses
she coaxes both cheeks with a blush the hue of a molten sunset
looks at the mirror
like she is staring into a fire—

"mija, beauty is pain,"
            she tells me

& I think she means the way   we girls
must learn to walk into   something burning

here, the old woman dressed in all black
tells me
"no andes aquí por la noche"   "do not pass by here
at night"

here, few of the girls make it to the party before midnight,
but here
death is a red tie event
too many of the girls get   chauffeured to

in which case,
my question becomes

is it not customary to prepare for the ball?

is it not like a woman to   pin her hair back
to make sure her edges are   sharp
to refuse to leave the house unless she is

ready?

they call me.

Immigrant Craft

the women in my family are master seamstresses for what they have
taught me to stitch together:

a blouse

            a curtain

                        a life.

Una Rosa Del Concreto

quisieron enterrarme
pero no pudieron
pararme

yo crecí
crecí
&
crecí

A Rose From Concrete

a rose from concrete
rose from the concrete
they wanted to bury me
but they couldn't keep me from growing

so I grew
& I grew

Call Me Mamasota

una mentalidad
a way of life
"take nothing from no one"

la mamasota no espera
la mamasota prospera
la mamasota intimida a los hombres
la mamasota es femenina
y masculina
es fuerte y suave
es poderosa y tierna

la mamasota se rifa
una fuerza de la naturaleza

They Call Me Calladita

"mira esta calladita"   look at this quiet girl

the man speaks of me   as if I am a show animal in a circus

expected to entertain   & failing all of my
requisitions

when I am loud   I watch the eyebrows raise
like velvet curtains

but oh how it makes   them squirm when I am quiet

oh how they sweat unsteadily   in their upholstered seats

how they would   love to know all that is happening
behind the stage

of my mind   sometimes

I do not have words   up there
but a production   instead

the assembly of hands   that are not my hands
turning cranks   swiftly   into story

moving memory into   porcelain boxes of tragedy & triumph

stretching moment into   memoir
past into   page

"why are you so quiet?"

they will prompt   &   how could you
explain the magnificence   of your silence?
better to make   them guess

better to let them   tremble   at your composure

calm, yes you are   but not like a statue   girl, no

calladita like a bomb   the moment awaiting

the storm

the breath   we all hold   before

the show begins.

Mamita

mamita, te juro que
este mundo está al revés

te convencen de que no vales
nada
y toda la belleza que tienes
ni la ves

mamita, por favor
no te fíes de las fotos
mejor te presto mis ojos
ahora verás
que todo es hermoso

Brujería

if I'm aligned with the cosmos
they think I've lost it

I think I'm cosmic

I think there is a voice
inside me that speaks
to all things,
that knows
the deepest truth
& I train myself to listen

they call this brujería,
I call it a language
between the stars & I
that only we
speak

they call me.

For the Girls with Long Names

I like to think of names as orgasms:
one is great,
but three-in-a-row is a blessing

esperanza-milagro aguilera, lina maría cañon, gladys teresa hidalgo

I like the names that introduce themselves

I like the names that wrap their lengthy letters around your strong
hand
and shake like they mean business

I like the names that get all dressed up to attend a party in their best
friend's kitchen

I like the names that bust open the door, bring their own music,
and demand the dJ play the song that sings to them

that even with their pushy insistence, their urgency to salsa
everywhere
somehow they remind you   every floor is waiting to be
made a stage,

why stay seated when you can fly? why have a body if not to turn it
into
an instrument?
the ones that tell you

"you think life is long,
but I have lost people, in less time than it takes to say my own name"

so these names pour wine into the teacups with their loud loud
laughs
and stretch out their pedicured syllables across your tongue

I have always been told my name is a   mouth-ful,
that I ought to trim the ends of its perfectly curled extensions,
but suddenly
I imagine god's writing process for names like ours.
I imagine god's jaw, unhinged on top of a
dictionary of adjectives

distraught, by the attempt to make a one-word title
for a thousand-page script

I like to think the longest names, the hardest-to-pronounce
names, the rolled letters and accent-heavy names,

in fact, are forewords to the memoirs most worth reading

and even the old white men professors and café baristas that
roll their eyes at the way you write yourself across a page
are secretly in awe of you,

how you make language a dance we do with our tongues,

how you give venacular a heartbeat,   how you make it known:

this name,   this breath,   this story,

will
                live
                        anyway.

they call me.

Struggle

when I really think about it,
to whom do I owe more thanks,
than the struggle?

than the storms that tested
my roots,
the turbulence that taught
me how to fly

it's the struggle that tested me,
that made me untouchable,
that shined a light on
everything that tried to stop me
& couldn't

it's the struggle that showed me
"look what you are made of"

"look at all that you have made of your life,
despite where you come from"

Diosa

durante mi noche oscura del alma
por un momento pensaba
que iba a morir del dolor

pero cuando me perdí
a la iglesia yo no fui

finalmente encontré
una diosa
en mi

Re-Introduction

how do you find the name for yourself,
when you have been given so many already?

I examine how the butterfly must enter a cocoon of silence
before she can spread her wings.

Zadie Smith wrote, "the past is always tense, the future perfect."

To begin, I burn all the books written of who I ought to be and I
move closer to the introduction.

I enter a cocoon so quiet I can only hear my own voice,

and on the other side of that cocoon, of that blazing library
of who I ought to be:

I emerge, brilliantly,
as me.

The woman I was always supposed to be.

angélica maria

About the author

Angélica Maria is an internationally touring poet and singer from Los Angeles. Her mestiza roots inspire her work that highlights femme narratives in Latinidad through both poetry and music. Her work has been featured on Facebook, Tedx, Button Poetry, and in 2021 she was contracted to write a poem for the USL National Women's Soccer League. She has presented at universities across the country including Pratt University in New York and Harvard University in Boston. She is a finalist of the National Poetry Slam 2018, Women of the World Poetry Slam 2019 and currently lives in Mexico City where she is creating her first EP of music in Spanglish, inspired by the divine feminine.

Email: angelicamalamaria@gmail.com
Instagram: @yosoyangelicamaria
Twitter: yosoyangmaria

CPSIA information can be obtained
at www.ICGtesting.com
Printed in the USA
LVHW070550090422
715655LV00001B/7